Cool Careers in Science

▸ **Creating the future of transportation**

▸ **Opportunities in engineering, design, and more**

▸ **Popular training paths**

DRIVERLESS
Vehicle Developers

ALTERNATIVE REALITY DEVELOPERS

ARTIFICIAL INTELLIGENCE SCIENTISTS

COMPUTER GAME & APP DEVELOPERS

DRIVERLESS VEHICLE DEVELOPERS

DRONE PILOTS

ENTERTAINMENT ENGINEERS

FORENSIC SCIENTISTS

PROFESSIONAL HACKERS

RENEWABLE ENERGY WORKERS

ROBOTICS DEVELOPERS

Cool Careers
in Science

DRIVERLESS
Vehicle
Developers

VOLKSWAGEN
GROUP

ANDREW MORKES

MC

MASON CREST
PHILADELPHIA
MIAMI

Mason Crest
450 Parkway Drive, Suite D
Broomall, Pennsylvania 19008
(866) MCP-BOOK (toll-free)

First printing

9 8 7 6 5 4 3 2 1

HARDBACK ISBN: 978-1-4222-4296-4
SERIES ISBN: 978-1-4222-4292-6
EBOOK ISBN: 978-1-4222-7513-9

Cataloging-in-Publication Data on file with the Library of Congress

Developed and Produced by National Highlights, Inc.
Interior and cover design: Jana Rade, impact studios
Interior layout: Annalisa Gumbrecht, Studio Gumbrecht
Production: Michelle Luke
Proofreader: Susan Uttendorfsky

QR CODES AND LINKS TO THIRD-PARTY CONTENT

Table of Contents

KEY ICONS TO LOOK FOR:

WORDS TO UNDERSTAND: These words with their easy-to-understand definitions will increase the reader's understanding of the text while building vocabulary skills.

SIDEBARS: This boxed material within the main text allows readers to build knowledge, gain insights, explore possibilities, and broaden their perspectives by weaving together additional information to provide realistic and holistic perspectives.

EDUCATIONAL VIDEOS: Readers can view videos by scanning our QR codes, providing them with additional educational content to supplement the text. Examples include news coverage, moments in history, speeches, iconic sports moments, and much more!

TEXT-DEPENDENT QUESTIONS: These questions send the reader back to the text for more careful attention to the evidence presented there.

RESEARCH PROJECTS: Readers are pointed toward areas of further inquiry connected to each chapter. Suggestions are provided for projects that encourage deeper research and analysis.

CAREERS IN SCIENCE OFFER GOOD PAY, THE OPPORTUNITY TO HELP PEOPLE, AND OTHER REWARDS

Where would we be without science? Well, we'd be without computers, smartphones, and other cutting-edge technologies. Crimes would take longer to solve without modern forensic analysis techniques. More of our private information would be stolen by hackers. We'd be stuck relying on environmentally unfriendly fossil fuels instead of using renewable energy. And life would be less fun because we wouldn't have drones; awe-inspiring and physics-defying roller coasters; the apps that we use to help us to stay fit, find directions, and get the news; and the computer and video games that we play for hours and hours.

Job markets are sometimes strong and sometimes weak, but a career in science (which, for the purposes of this series, includes the related fields of technology and engineering) is almost a sure path to a comfortable life. The following paragraphs provide more information on why a career in science is a great choice.

Good pay. People in science careers earn some of the highest salaries in the work world. Median annual salaries for those in computer and mathematical careers in the United States are $84,575, according to the U.S. Department of Labor (USDL). This is much higher than the median earnings ($37,690) for all careers. Additionally, those in life, physical, and social science occupations can earn $64,510, and those in engineering careers earn $79,180. Science professionals who become managers or who launch their own businesses can earn anywhere from $150,000 to $300,000 or more.

Strong employment prospects. There are shortages of science workers throughout the world, according to the consulting firm ManpowerGroup. In fact, engineering workers are the third most in demand occupational field in the world. Technicians rank fourth, and computer and information technology professionals rank sixth.

There's a shortage of software engineers in more than twenty countries, including in the United States, Canada, Mexico, Japan, and the United Kingdom, according to the recruitment firm Michael Page. Other science careers where there is a shortage of workers include electronics engineers (nineteen countries), electrical engineers (sixteen countries), data analysts (eleven countries), and hardware engineers (six countries), among other workers.

The USDL predicts that employment of computer and information technology professionals in the United States will grow by 13 percent during the next decade. Career opportunities for those in life, physical, and social science occupations will grow by 10 percent. Both of these career fields are growing faster than the average for all careers. The outlook is also good for engineering professionals. Employment is expected to grow by 7 percent during the next decade. The strongest opportunities will be found in renewable energy and robotics.

By 2026, the USDL predicts that there will be more than 876,000 new jobs in science, technology, engineering, and mathematics fields.

Rewarding work environment and many career options. A career in science is fulfilling because you get to use both your creative and practical sides to develop new technologies (or improve existing ones), solve problems, and make the world a better place. There's a common misconception that science workers spend most of their time in dreary, windowless laboratories or offices. While they do spend lots of time in the laboratory or offices, they also spend time in the field, testing, troubleshooting, and trying out their inventions or discoveries. Some science professionals launch their own businesses, which can be both fun and very rewarding.

Job opportunities are available throughout the United States and the world. Science professionals play such an important role in our modern world that there are jobs almost anywhere, although many positions are found in big cities.

IS A CAREER IN SCIENCE RIGHT FOR ME?

Test your interest. How many of these statements do you agree with?

____ My favorite classes in school are computer- and science-related.

____ I like to learn about scientific breakthroughs.

____ I like to use technology to solve problems.

____ I like to build and fix things.

____ I enjoy doing science experiments.

____ I am curious about how things work.

____ I enjoy writing computer code.

____ I like to invent things.

____ I have a good imagination.

____ I like to build electronics and other things that require electricity.

____ I am good at math.

If many of the statements above describe you, then you should consider a career in the sciences. But you don't need to select a career right now. Check out this book on a career as a driverless vehicle developer, and other books in the series, to learn more about occupational paths in the sciences and related fields. Good luck with your career exploration!

WORDS TO UNDERSTAND

artificial neural network (ANN): biological brain–inspired systems that are created to replicate the way that humans learn; they consist of layers of connected "neurons" that share information; also known as **connectionist systems**

automated driving features: those that are incorporated into semi-autonomous and autonomous vehicles to perform tasks without the assistance of the human driver; they include traffic jam chauffeur and local driverless taxi features; additionally, brake and gas pedals and the steering wheel may not be installed

car insurance: financial protection against certain risks such as damage to one's vehicle or the vehicles of others, damage to personal property, and injury to drivers, passengers, or pedestrians

driver support features: those that are incorporated into vehicles to perform automated tasks under the supervision of human drivers; these include automatic emergency braking, blind spot warning, lane departure warning, and adaptive cruise control technology; also known as **advanced driver assistance systems**

Silicon Valley: A region that is located at the south end of San Francisco Bay in California that is the home to many startup and global technology companies

Chapter 1

DRIVERLESS VEHICLES AND CAREER PATHS

WHAT ARE DRIVERLESS VEHICLES?

What was once science fiction has become reality. Driverless vehicles are now being tested on roads all over the world. These vehicles employ a wide range of technologies to help them safely navigate city streets and highways without a human driver. Driverless vehicles are also known as "self-driving vehicles" and "autonomous vehicles."

The term "driverless vehicle" is actually misleading because no vehicle is currently available for sale that can drive without the assistance of a human driver to some degree. A fully driverless vehicle that is available to the public is perhaps ten, or even twenty years away, but predictions vary greatly. A better way to classify these computer-driven vehicles is by their level of autonomy (the number of actions something can perform without oversight). A semi-autonomous vehicle is one that can do some tasks without human control, or one that can drive for a period of time before a human driver must retake control. An autonomous vehicle is one that can drive without human control.

Lidar

Pedestrian Detection

Lane Change Assist

Blind Spot
Detection

A simulation
of how LiDAR
works.

Driverless vehicles rely on the following technologies:

- **Cameras:** These optical devices are used to view and pass along information on lane markings, traffic lights, pedestrians, other vehicles, road signs, and other objects in or near the road.

- **LiDAR:** Short for Light Detection And Ranging, LiDAR is a type of active remote sensing technology that sends millions of beams of light energy (laser) every second to an area around the vehicle until it hits objects and bounces back to a sensor. It is used to build a 3-D map that tells the vehicle where humans and objects are located in relation to it.

- **RADAR:** Stands for RAdio Detecting And Ranging. This technology sends out radio waves that are reflected back by objects in their path. RADAR is used to detect the presence of an object at a distance, detect the speed of an object, or map something.

- **Sensors:** This technology detects environmental conditions and provides information to the vehicle's operating systems so that it can analyze and react to road conditions.

- **Artificial intelligence (AI):** AI is the simulation of human intelligence (perceiving, reasoning, learning, problem-solving, etc.) by machinery and computer systems. AI-enabled machinery and computer systems do so by collecting (via cameras and sensors) and assessing vast amounts of information as a vehicle travels along a street or highway. Deep learning, a subspecialty of AI, is used to create behavioral models that help the computer to learn how to react to a variety of road situations (heavy traffic, a pedestrian crossing the road, etc.) and conditions (daylight, night driving, snow, rain, etc.). As it gathers information and learns from its mistakes, the computer improves its performance level.

DID YOU KNOW?

Alphabet's driverless car company Waymo recently announced that its vehicles have driven a collective 10 million miles (16,093,440 kilometers) on U.S. roads.

It's estimated that hundreds of automotive, tech, and transportation network companies are currently developing driverless vehicles or related technology. This group includes General Motors, BMW, Waymo, Uber, Lyft, Toyota, Tesla, NVIDIA, Intel, Samsung Semiconductor, Lucid Motors, Honda, Hyundai, Kia, Jaguar, Mazda, Mitsubishi, Ford Motors, Nissan, Audi, Aurora, and Baidu.

By 2025, the worldwide market for partially autonomous vehicles is expected to reach $36 billion, according to Statista.com. In this same year, the market

A Waymo self-driving car.

for fully autonomous vehicles is expected to hit $6 billion. "Self-driving and electric cars will help create more than 100,000 U.S. mobility industry jobs in the coming decade, including up to 30,000 jobs for engineers with degrees in computer-related subjects," according to research from Boston Consulting Group and Detroit Mobility Lab.

The U.S. automotive industry has been typically concentrated in Detroit, Michigan, but opportunities in the driverless vehicle industry are available across the country. Companies that are located in **Silicon Valley** offer the largest number of jobs, according to a study of employment postings by Indeed.com. Detroit was a close second, followed by San Francisco, California, and Pittsburgh, Pennsylvania. Boston, Massachusetts, also hosts a variety of companies and colleges and universities that conduct research in the field.

COUNTRIES THAT ARE MOST READY FOR DRIVERLESS VEHICLES

The professional services firm KPMG conducted a study to determine which nations were most ready for driverless vehicles. Countries that ranked high have excellent road infrastructure, a supportive government, and residents who are enthusiastic about this technology. Here are the rankings:

1. Netherlands
2. Singapore
3. United States
4. Sweden
5. United Kingdom
6. Germany
7. Canada
8. United Arab Emirates
9. New Zealand
10. South Korea
11. Japan
12. Austria
13. France
14. Australia
15. Spain
16. China
17. Brazil
18. Russia
19. Mexico
20. India

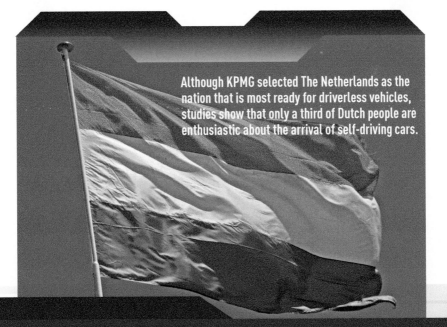

Although KPMG selected The Netherlands as the nation that is most ready for driverless vehicles, studies show that only a third of Dutch people are enthusiastic about the arrival of self-driving cars.

Learn more about the five levels of autonomy for self-driving cars and the pros and cons of this technology

LEVELS OF AUTONOMOUS DRIVING

SAE International, a professional association for engineers and technical experts, has created a Levels of Driving Automation standard that defines the levels of driving automation. In Levels 0–2, autonomous support features are available, but the driver is still in control of the vehicle even if their hands are not on the wheel and their feet are temporarily off the pedals. In Levels 3–5, the driver is not driving when these features are engaged. Each higher level involves less human driver operation and supervision and more autonomous operation. Here is more information on the levels:

Level 0: Driver support features such as automatic emergency braking, blind spot warning, and lane departure warning systems are available, but limited to providing the driver with warnings and momentary assistance.

Level 1: Driver support features such as lane departure warnings or adaptive cruise control technology are available, but not at the same time.

Level 2: Driver support features such as lane departure warnings, remote-controlled parking, collision avoidance braking, and adaptive cruise control technology are available at the same time.

Level 3: Automated driving features (ADFs) such as traffic jam chauffeur are available, but the human driver must take over in a matter of seconds when the system requests assistance. For Levels 3 and 4, ADFs will only operate if all required conditions are met.

Level 4: ADFs such as local driverless taxi are available, and the cockpit (steering wheel, brake and gas pedals, gearbox, etc.) may or may not be installed. The computer will not ask the driver to take over.

Level 5: All Level 4 ADFs are in place, there is no cockpit, and the vehicle can drive autonomously anywhere and in all conditions. Anyone riding in the car is simply a passenger.

REAR CAMERA

SELF DRIVING

A self-driving electric truck on a road.

PUBLIC OPINION REGARDING AUTONOMOUS VEHICLES

It's not surprising that public opinion varies significantly regarding driverless vehicles. Human-driven vehicles have been around for more than 120 years, so it's a little hard to fathom a computer taking over and driving a car. Plus, recent incidents in which driverless vehicles killed or injured pedestrians have tested the public's faith in this new technology. Here are the results of three surveys regarding driverless vehicles:

Seventy-five percent of drivers surveyed by the Consumer Technology Association in 2016 said that they were excited about the many benefits offered by driverless vehicles. Sixty percent were interested in swapping their car for a self-driving one. Those surveyed said that the top potential benefits of self-driving cars were reduced aggressive and drunk driving accidents, the opportunity to reduce car insurance costs, and new mobility options for people with disabilities.

In 2016, 70 percent of Australians surveyed by the Australia and New Zealand Driverless Vehicle Initiative (ANZDVI) said that they would want a driverless vehicle to take over for them if they felt tired or bored.

In 2018, 73 percent of American drivers surveyed by the American Automobile Association said that they would be too afraid to ride in a fully self-driving vehicle.

THE PROS AND CONS OF DRIVERLESS VEHICLES

Just like any new technology, driverless vehicles have their positives and negatives. For example, scientists believe that the use of self-driving cars will reduce the number of accidents, but considerable research, development, and troubleshooting are still needed before these systems can be completely trusted to replace a human driver. Automotive experts are also concerned with developing self-driving vehicle software that cannot be hacked (taken control of via electronic means) by criminals to steal the vehicle or make the car crash into other vehicles. The following sections provide more information on the potential advantages and disadvantages of driverless vehicles.

BENEFITS OF DRIVERLESS TECHNOLOGY

The introduction of driverless vehicles will change the way we live and work. For example, cities may be redesigned to become more pedestrian- and cyclist-friendly. Driverless vehicles may be used as mobile offices, stores (including supermarkets), and even hotel rooms, allowing companies to provide goods and services to customers more quickly. Here are some other expected benefits of driverless vehicles.

REDUCED TRAFFIC DEATHS

Motor vehicle crashes on U.S. highways claim nearly 40,000 lives a year, according to the U.S. Department of Transportation. Ninety-four percent of serious vehicle crashes are caused by human error. The introduction of driverless vehicles is expected to greatly reduce the number of deaths and injuries that are caused by traffic accidents (including those caused by drunk drivers). In addition to a reduction in the loss of human life, the use of

The introduction of driverless vehicles is expected to greatly decrease the number of traffic accidents.

self-driving vehicles will also lower the financial costs of these accidents. For example, road crashes cost Australia $27 billion annually, according to the ANZDVI. This number could be significantly reduced if autonomous and semi-autonomous vehicles were introduced.

IMPROVED MOBILITY FOR THE ELDERLY AND THOSE WITH DISABILITIES

Fully automated vehicles will allow these groups to increase their independence and allow them better access to education, health-care services, and the basics of human life (grocery shopping, visits with friends and family, etc.). Their introduction could also create job opportunities for people with disabilities. A study referenced by the National Highway Traffic Safety Administration estimates that the use of driverless vehicles could create approximately 2 million new jobs for people with disabilities.

SAVING TIME AND IMPROVING PRODUCTIVITY FOR COMMUTERS

It's estimated that Americans spend an entire week stuck in in traffic annually. That's a lot of wasted time. The use of fully automated vehicles will allow drivers to get this time back. As they lounge in the backseat, they will be able to sleep, catch up on work, read a book or watch a movie, or simply relax and watch the scenery go by.

JOB GAINS

The introduction of driverless vehicles will create new jobs for engineers, technicians, artificial intelligence scientists, industrial designers, sales professionals, and mechanics who have specialized expertise in the repair of software, RADAR, sensors, cameras, and LiDAR. (On the other hand, the use of self-driving vehicles will also cause job losses in other fields. I'll cover that issue a little bit later in this chapter.)

REDUCED ROAD CONGESTION AND POLLUTION

Some experts believe that the number of vehicles on roads will decline as more people forego paying tens of thousands of dollars to purchase their own cars and trucks and paying for insurance and maintenance costs. Instead, they will utilize car-share programs or take advantage of taxis or services such as Lyft or Uber. If this occurs, roads will be less congested, allowing people to get to their destinations faster than they had in the past as automated vehicles work together to smooth traffic flow. Easing congestion will also create less pollution, which will improve the health of tens of millions of people with respiratory diseases.

DAY IN THE LIFE: AUTONOMOUS VEHICLE TESTER

If someone asked me to describe my job as a driverless vehicle tester in three words, I'd say, "Exciting, challenging, rewarding."

My job is exciting because I'm a total car geek, and it's really awesome to be able to test cutting-edge technology that almost no one else has experienced. The first time you're behind the wheel of a driverless vehicle, it will blow your mind. The wheel turns and the car accelerates and brakes, all without you ever touching the wheel or pedals. Your muscle memory as a driver keeps telling you to grab the wheel and brake or hit the gas, when appropriate, but then you realize that the car has everything under control—at least mostly. That's where my job starts.

It's challenging because I must pay close attention to the operation of the vehicle during each test. I sit in the driver's seat with my foot hovering over the brake pedal and hands close to the wheel in order to be ready at any moment to take control of the vehicle. But that's just one part of my job. During the test, I'm ready to take over, but I'm also tasked with gathering information to provide feedback to the engineering and software teams. Depending on the specific test, I might be asked to provide information that answers the following questions: Is the vehicle accelerating and braking in a timely fashion? Does the vehicle respond quickly to verbal commands from a passenger? Is it stopping at the appropriate location at stoplights and other settings? This technology is not yet perfected, so the car does occasionally make mistakes, such as stopping short of an intersection at a red light, then slowly inching forward to the proper line. I take notes on all these issues, writing them up in reports that I begin when the vehicle stops at a red light, and then complete once my shift (six to eight hours) is over. At some companies I've worked at, I've worked in a two-person team, with one person behind the wheel and another in the passenger seat, taking notes on a laptop, recording the car's road performance, and monitoring data feeds from the car's sensors.

Working as a test driver is rewarding because my work directly impacts the development of the autonomous vehicle industry. I'm helping to make these vehicles safe for the public. When I'm old and gray and driverless vehicles are as commonplace as traditional cars and trucks are today, I can say that I was there at the beginning and played a small, but important, role in their creation.

Take a ride in Waymo's self-driving car

DRAWBACKS OF DRIVERLESS TECHNOLOGY

Many good things will happen once autonomous vehicles are in wide use, but there are also negative possibilities that the industry and politicians will need to address. The following paragraphs provide more information on these issues.

JOB LOSSES

Although the introduction of self-driving vehicles will generate new jobs, it will also cause major job losses in some employment sectors. The Center for Global Policy Solutions estimates that more than 4 million jobs (mostly in taxi, delivery, truck, and bus driving) in the U.S. alone will be lost if there is a rapid transition to autonomous vehicles. Drivers that use vehicles on highways will be most affected because driverless technology operates more easily in this environment. As a result, workers will need to be retrained to work in other positions, although some people may not be able to find jobs that offer the same pay as they received while working as truckers, bus drivers, and in other transportation careers.

RISK OF INJURY TO PEOPLE AND DAMAGE TO PROPERTY

Driverless vehicle technology still has a long way to go before it can be considered safe for a car's occupants, those in other cars, and pedestrians. There have been some high-profile incidents in which self-driving vehicles have crashed into buildings, flipped over in accidents, and struck, and even killed, pedestrians. In 2018 an experimental Uber autonomous vehicle hit and killed a pedestrian in Arizona. This was the first fatal accident of its kind. If these types of incidents continue to occur, the public may lose interest in using driverless vehicles.

CYBERSECURITY

Hackers have already proven that they can hack (break into) the computer systems of conventional vehicles, and this is an even a bigger concern for autonomous vehicles. If a hacker manages to get control of a vehicle, they could force it to stop working, to crash into other cars, to hit pedestrians, or to drive off the road into walls and lakes, or off cliffs. This is a scary thought, and scientists and computer security professionals will need to develop top-notch digital security systems to protect driverless vehicles from hackers.

INCREASED POLLUTION

Some experts believe that the introduction of driverless vehicles will prompt more people to use automated cars and trucks, which will increase air, soil, and water pollution levels if vehicles with petroleum-burning engines are still used. To reduce pollution, policy experts recommend the introduction of more "green vehicles" that use electric power, hydrogen, compressed natural gas, ethanol, or biodiesel (although some environmentalists do not believe all these fuels can be classified as "green"). Experts also recommend that more emphasis be placed on car-sharing and carpooling to reduce the number of vehicles that are on the road.

Some people believe that the introduction of driverless vehicles will actually prompt more people to use cars, which would cause more air pollution.

EMPLOYERS OF DRIVERLESS VEHICLE DEVELOPERS

- Traditional automakers
- Alternative energy vehicle makers
- Tech companies that are developing driverless technology
- Colleges and universities
- Military
- Any company or organization that is developing support technology or systems that are used in driverless vehicles

CAREER PATHS IN DRIVERLESS VEHICLE DEVELOPMENT

People with many different educational backgrounds work in driverless vehicle development: artificial intelligence, programming, robotics, software development, computer security, mathematics, engineering, science, and industrial design. This is true because a variety of skills and knowledge areas are required to design, build, test, and troubleshoot and revise the software, hardware, and systems that comprise driverless vehicles. Let's take a look at some specific career paths in the self-driving vehicle industry.

COMPUTER AND ENGINEERING CAREERS

Software developers write the software that's used to operate driverless vehicles. This software is utilized for everything from operating cameras and sensors to code that allows a vehicle to collect information about its environment and respond to stimuli.

AI powers the "brains" of the vehicle. Major subspecialties in AI include machine learning, deep learning, and computer vision. Machine-learning engineers are experts in data science, applied research, **artificial neural networks (ANNs)**, coding, collaborative tools (such as GitHub), and programming languages (especially Python, C, C++, and Java). They create programs and algorithms that allow machines and software to perform actions with little or no oversight by humans. An algorithm is a list of rules or guidelines to follow in order to solve a problem or complete a task. In the computer field, algorithms tell computer hardware or software what to do, with three logical operations: AND, OR, and NOT. Machine-learning algorithms change their actions based on new information that is gathered.

Deep learning is a more complex type of machine learning in which ANNs have many layers of connected "neurons." *Deep-learning engineers:*

- Analyze and optimize deep-learning and machine-learning models, algorithms, and applications

- Design, develop and optimize machine-learning kernels and algorithms for deep-learning accelerators

- Study deep-learning models to identify performance bottlenecks and propose solutions

Computer vision is an AI specialty in which machines (including autonomous vehicles) are taught how to view and interpret the world around them. *Computer vision*

An engineer tests a vehicle's software.

engineers and scientists use mathematical concepts (geometry, linear algebra, numerical methods), machine learning, and other types of AI to design and develop optical systems and image processing algorithms for 2–D and 3–D applications. Multiple cameras are incorporated into driverless vehicles to gather a variety of information. They are used to estimate road curvature, find lanes, detect and classify traffic signs and lights, identify obstacles, and more. In the driverless vehicle industry, the use of computer vision is sometimes referred to as "perception." Cameras are a very useful component in driverless vehicles, but they aren't good at collecting information on and estimating distance, height, and the velocity (speed) of other objects, so RADAR and LiDAR are often used to record these measurements.

Natural language processing (NLP) focuses on teaching computers to understand, interpret, and manipulate written and spoken human languages. Computers can be taught to understand, summarize, and translate basic language, but they don't have the human ability to understand what some words or sentences really mean. *NLP engineers* and *scientists* help design, develop, train, and maintain NLP models that teach computers to correctly understand language and decipher challenging language riddles. NLP systems in driverless vehicles are extremely important because miscommunication between the computer and passenger could result in delays in getting to a destination or perhaps even an accident if, for some reason, the AI system has a severe malfunction.

Mechanical engineers research, design, and develop mechanical and electro-mechanical devices or systems of driverless vehicles.

Electrical engineers design, build, and troubleshoot the electrical systems that store, generate, or deliver energy to autonomous systems or entire vehicles (if they are powered by electricity). *Electronics engineers* help design electronic components, software, or systems.

Mechatronics engineers use their knowledge of electronics, mechanics, computers, and control engineering to develop driverless vehicles and other types of robots.

Hardware engineers design and build mechanical or electrical components and systems. They test and debug newly assembled systems and make improvements to existing designs.

Industrial engineers identify ways to reduce waste, improve the efficiency of systems and work processes, and increase worker productivity during the development and manufacturing of driverless vehicles.

Engineering technicians and *technologists* help engineers and scientists design, develop, test, and troubleshoot driverless vehicles and other robotics technology. They perform less complicated tasks so that engineers and scientists can work on "big picture" issues, or complex design or repair challenges.

OTHER CAREER PATHS

Driverless vehicle mechanics repair damaged or malfunctioning autonomous and semi-autonomous cars, trucks, buses, and other vehicles. They have specialized knowledge of mechanical design, electronics, electrical systems, RADAR, LiDAR, sensors, cameras, basic software design, and other aspects of engineering and science and technologies.

Computer security is a big concern of driverless vehicle developers. *Professional hackers* stop cybercriminals from hacking into self-driving cars and committing other cybercrimes. They are also known as *white hat hackers, ethical hackers,* and *information security analysts* (although people with this job title many have other non-hacking duties).

An automotive engineer tests a vehicle during the manufacturing process.

Once fully autonomous cars are perfected, these vehicles will no longer have a steering wheel, brake and gas pedals, gearbox, and other components used by human drivers. As a result, the exterior and interior of these new autonomous vehicles will need to be redesigned. Semi-autonomous vehicles are also being redesigned so that there is better communication between the car and the driver. *Industrial designers* use their knowledge of art, engineering, physics, and computer-aided design (CAD) to create these vehicles.

User interface and experience designers, who are sometimes called *interaction designers*, *human-machine interface (HMI) designers*, and *interface designers*, focus on the technology in driverless vehicles that allows drivers and passengers to communicate with the computer. HMIs may incorporate touchscreen displays, voice recognition software, or technology that allows for integration with mobile devices. It's important that passengers can easily use driverless vehicle technology and be understood by the computer as it drives. Since the public still has concerns about giving up control of their vehicles, designers are developing communication and/or signaling systems that will reassure passengers that the computer is functioning and that it has identified potential safety hazards, such as a merging vehicle or a pedestrian. At some companies, they are also developing systems that communicate with passengers in other cars and with pedestrians.

Autonomous and *semi-autonomous vehicle testers*, who are also known as *driverless vehicle test operators*, monitor the systems in the vehicle during test drives on public and private roads. For semi-autonomous vehicle assessments, they sit in the driver's seat and observe the vehicle as it navigates city streets, highways, or test tracks. They must be ready to quickly take over if problems arise during testing. During all trials, these professionals follow a plan provided by engineers and scientists. When the analysis is finished, testers prepare reports that provide detailed feedback to the engineering team on assessment results and vehicle performance.

TEXT-DEPENDENT QUESTIONS:

1. What is LiDAR?
2. Can you name three potential benefits of driverless vehicles?
3. What are three career paths in the field?

RESEARCH PROJECT:

Get started exploring the world of driverless technology by building a miniature self-driving car. Visit www.youtube.com/watch?v=cB_ez2MNHMo to learn how to build this type of vehicle. Plenty of other websites offer tips on building a self-driving car. Ask your friends to help you with this project, and demonstrate your car in science or shop class.

Chapter 2

TERMS OF THE TRADE

active sensor: A sensor that is designed to instigate an action and then wait for a response in order to collect information.

advanced driver assistance systems: Vehicle systems—such as adaptive cruise control and forward collision warning—that are designed to improve driving safety.

aftermarket technology: Equipment that is installed after the purchase of a vehicle.

algorithm: A list of rules or guidelines to follow in order to solve a problem or complete a task. Examples of algorithms used in regular life include a recipe that is used to bake a cake or directions to find a destination. In the computer field, algorithms are used to tell computer hardware or software what to do, with three logical operations: AND, OR, and NOT. Machine-learning algorithms change their actions based on new information that is gathered. These actions can sometimes be unpredictable and negative.

artificial intelligence (AI): The simulation of human intelligence (perceiving, reasoning, learning, problem-solving, etc.) by machinery and computer systems.

artificial intelligence accelerator: A specialized microchip that is designed to enable faster processing of AI tasks.

artificial neural network (ANN): Biological brain–inspired systems that are created to replicate the way that humans learn. They consist of layers of connected "neurons" that share information. ANNs are one of the main tools used in machine learning. They are also known as **connectionist systems**.

augmented reality: A computer-generated system that combines a virtual environment with imaginary elements that are introduced to a real environment; examples include Snapchat lenses and the game *Pokémon Go*.

automated driving features (ADFs): Those that are incorporated into semi-autonomous and autonomous vehicles to perform tasks without the assistance of the human driver. They include traffic jam chauffeur and local driverless taxi features. Additionally, brake and gas pedals and the steering wheel may not be installed in vehicles that incorporate automated driving features.

autonomous vehicle: One that can drive without human control.

axle: A central shaft that connects to two wheels on a vehicle.

battery: A rechargeable component that stores and provides the electrical power that is required to start an engine; it also powers vehicle accessories, such as the radio, when the engine is not running.

biofuel-powered vehicles: Cars, trucks, and other vehicles that are powered by plant materials that are converted into liquid fuels. One popular biofuel is ethanol, which is made from sugars found in grains such as corn, barley, sorghum, and rice, as well as from sugarcane, sugar beets, potato skins, yard clippings, tree bark, and switchgrass.

brakes: Mechanical devices that slow or stop a car if the driver presses the brake pedal with their foot, or if an automated vehicle directs the car to slow or stop.

cameras: Visual recording devices that are built into autonomous and semi-autonomous vehicles. The cameras work in concert with computer vision technology to spot lane lines, traffic lights, speed limit signs, and other signs and objects along the road so that the vehicle can operate correctly.

car insurance: Financial protection against certain risks such as damage to one's vehicle or the vehicles of others, damage to personal property, and injury to drivers, passengers, or pedestrians.

cloud computing: Computer services that are provided over the internet instead of on a personal computer or local server. Sometimes referred to as **the cloud.**

code: Instructions that tell a computer what to do.

collision avoidance system: Technology that is used to reduce the severity of or prevent an accident. These systems use RADAR, LiDAR, lasers, cameras, and sometimes Global Positioning System sensors to detect and alert drivers to potential dangers and, in some vehicles, take action (braking, steering, or both) autonomously without any driver input.

computer-aided design (CAD): The process of using software to create architectural plans, blueprints, or artwork.

computer vision: An AI specialty in which machines are taught how to view and interpret the world around them.

connected vehicle: A vehicle that is equipped with a wireless communication device that allows it to communicate with other vehicles on the road, roadside infrastructure, other travelers, and the cloud.

cybersecurity: The process of protecting computers and related technology from attacks from cybercriminals.

deep learning: A more complex type of machine learning in which ANNs have many layers of connected "neurons."

driver support features: Features that are incorporated into vehicles that perform automated tasks under the supervision of human drivers. These include automatic emergency braking, blind spot warning, lane departure warning, lane centering, and adaptive cruise control technology. Also known as **advanced driver assistance systems**.

electrical engineering: The use of scientific and engineering principles to develop and build electrical systems such as electric motors, radar and navigation systems, and power generation equipment.

electronics engineering: The use of scientific and engineering principles to develop and build electronic equipment, such as broadcast and communications systems.

engineering: The use of science and engineering principles to design, build, test, troubleshoot, and repair products, systems, and structures.

far infrared sensor: A sensor that detects a heat profile of living things in low or even zero light situations in order to identify the presence of pedestrians or animals on or near the road at nighttime, or in other instances in which visibility is poor.

frameworks: Proprietary or open-source software tools that allow programmers and scientists to develop and utilize artificial intelligence in a variety of ways. Some popular machine-learning frameworks include Spark ML, TensorFlow, Caffe, Torch, and Mahout.

fuel cell: A fuel cell is a mechanical device that works like a battery but that does not run down or need recharging. Fuel cells use the chemical energy of hydrogen or another fuel to cleanly and efficiently produce electricity.

Global Positioning System (GPS): A satellite-based navigation system established by the U.S. Department of Defense that is made up of at least twenty-four satellites. Driverless vehicles have a GPS system built in that allows them to track their position/location in relation to these satellites.

graphical processing unit: A specialized electronic circuit that provides the computing power to perform many AI processes.

hacker: The term for both people who seek to use their computer and hacking skills to do good, and those who use their talents to do bad.

hardware: The physical components that make up a computer system.

hardware engineering: The use of scientific and engineering principles to research, design, develop, and test actuators, processors, circuit boards, networks, routers, memory devices, and other types of technology.

human-computer interaction: The study of the interaction between humans and computers. The integration of AI (natural language processing, computer vision, neurotechnology, etc.) into computers has opened up many new avenues of study in the field.

human-computer interface: In a driverless vehicle, the interface that allows for two-way communication between a vehicle and its occupants.

The interface may incorporate voice recognition software, touchscreen displays, or technology that enables integration with mobile devices.

hybrid electric vehicles: Vehicles that often look like regular cars and trucks but that usually have an electric motor and a small internal combustion engine (ICE). They are powered by two energy sources: an energy storage device (such as a battery pack) and an energy conversion unit (such as a fuel cell or combustion engine). Hybrid electric vehicles offer better fuel economy and produce less pollution than ICE vehicles do.

Internet of Things (IoT): A network of appliances, vehicles, etc., that are embedded with electronics, sensors, software, and other technology that allows them to communicate with each other and share information.

Internet of Vehicles (IoV): A network of vehicles that consists of three networks: an inter-vehicle network, an intra-vehicle network, and a vehicular mobile network.

LiDAR: Short for Light Detection and Ranging. LiDAR is a type of active remote sensing technology that sends millions of beams of light energy (laser) every second to an area around the vehicle until it hits objects and bounces back to a sensor. It is used to build a 3-D map that tells the vehicle where humans and objects are located in relation to it. LiDAR is a key component of autonomous and semi-autonomous vehicles.

machine intelligence: An umbrella term that covers classical learning algorithms, machine learning, and deep learning.

machine learning: A branch of AI that involves programming and teaching systems to learn from data, identify patterns, and make decisions with little human intervention.

maps: In relation to autonomous and semi-autonomous vehicles, plans that are created by cameras and LiDAR before a vehicle takes to the streets. The maps provide guidance to the vehicle and allow it to verify its sensor readings.

mechanical engineering: A broad engineering discipline that uses scientific and engineering principles to design and oversee the manufacture of a wide variety of products and systems, including electric generators, refrigeration and air-conditioning systems, elevators and

escalators, amusement park rides, internal combustion engines, fuel cells, and gas-electric hybrid engines.

mechatronics: A field of engineering that combines mechanical, control, computer, electrical, and communication engineering.

microcontroller: Technology that controls all the systems in a mechanical device.

microprocessor: An integrated circuit that is used to perform key functions in a computer.

mobile devices: Smartphones, tablet computers, e-readers, and wearable technology.

natural language processing (NLP): A sub-area of AI that focuses on teaching computers to understand, interpret, and manipulate written and spoken human language.

network: A group of computers that are linked to accomplish a goal.

open-source software: A type of software that is free and which anyone can inspect, modify, and improve the code that makes it work. Some developers use open-source software when working on AI projects.

partially automated driving systems: Technology—such as GPS navigation and driver warning systems—that assists humans as they drive.

pattern recognition: A branch of machine learning that focuses on the recognition of patterns and regularities in data in order to obtain information about a system or data set. Also known as **pattern analysis**.

passive sensor: A sensor that is designed to "listen" for information rather than actively send out a signal and record the response.

platooning: A method of grouping semi-autonomous and autonomous vehicles together on the road to increase road capacity and efficiency. The goal of platooning is to decrease the distances between vehicles and allow them to accelerate or brake simultaneously, thus allowing traffic to move more smoothly.

plug-in hybrid vehicles: This type of vehicle features both a battery pack and a combustion engine that uses gasoline or another type of fuel. It uses electricity for short trips and uses liquid fuel for longer trips. Unlike a standard hybrid electric vehicle with a battery, drivers can recharge this type of car by taking it to a recharging station or simply plugging it into an electrical outlet in their garage.

programmer: A person who writes computer code that tells computers what to do and how to react in a specific situation.

programming code: Instructions that tell hardware and software what to do. Also called **programming language**.

proprietary software: A type of software that is owned and controlled by the person or company that developed it.

RADAR: Stands for RAdio Detecting And Ranging. A technology that sends out radio waves that are reflected back by objects in their path. RADAR is used to detect the presence of an object at a distance, detect the speed of an object, or to map something.

reinforcement learning: A type of machine-learning method in which an algorithm learns by interacting with its environment. During this process, the algorithm is either rewarded or penalized. This teaches it how to make decisions that maximize rewards over time.

robot: A self-controlled machine that is designed to perform tasks more efficiently and less expensively than can be done by humans and to perform other functions. They are usually equipped with appendages that allow them to move and interact with their environment. The word "robot" comes from the Czech word *robota*, which means "forced work."

robotics: An interdisciplinary area of science and mechanical, electronic engineering, computer, and other types of engineering. Those involved in the field of robotics create robots that are used to perform tasks more efficiently and less expensively than can be done by humans. A driverless vehicle is a type of robot.

semi-autonomous vehicle: One that can perform some tasks without human control, or that can drive for a period of time before a human driver must retake control.

sensor: Technology that detects environmental conditions and provides information to humans or a robot.

smart-enabled road infrastructure: Electronics built into traffic signals, stoplights, speed limit signs, barriers, and message boards, as well as sensors embedded in the pavement, that collect and send information and communicate with driverless vehicles.

software engineering: The use of scientific and engineering principles to design software applications, software that operates computer and other systems, and other types of software.

software: A program that operates a computer or allows a user to perform a specific task.

touch sensor: A sensor that measures an aspect of its physical contact with an object.

traffic jam chauffeur: Technology developed by the PSA Groupe that enables a car to operate autonomously during traffic jams with no supervision required. The car automatically adapts its speed to that of the speed limit and surrounding traffic.

transmission: A component in a vehicle that takes the energy generated by the engine and transmits it to the connected wheels to move the vehicle.

vehicle-to-infrastructure communication: The exchange of information between driverless vehicles and infrastructure.

vehicle-to-vehicle communication: The exchange of information between driverless vehicles.

vehicle-to-X communication: Pronounced "vehicle to many." The exchange of information between driverless vehicles and infrastructure, various internet applications, and traffic management centers.

virtual reality (VR): A computer-generated experience that takes place within a simulated environment using headgear or other equipment that shuts out the real world.

virus: A type of malware that is typically hidden in a software program or computer file; it must be downloaded or forwarded for it to be activated.

visual sensor: A device, typically a camera, that obtains a visual representation of something.

WORDS TO UNDERSTAND

apprenticeship: a formal training program that combines classroom instruction and supervised practical experience; apprentices are paid a salary that increases as they obtain experience

base salary: the amount a person gets paid each year for doing their job

bonus: money awarded by an employer to a worker at the end of the year if they performed exceptionally well on the job

certificate: a credential that shows a person has completed specialized education, passed a test, and met other requirements to qualify for work in a career or industry; college certificate programs typically last six months to a year

profit sharing: a policy established by some companies in which it awards a small amount of the money it earned during the last year to its employees

Chapter 3

PREPARING FOR THE FIELD AND MAKING A LIVING

EDUCATIONAL PATHS

You'll need at least a bachelor's degree (a four-year degree that one completes after high school), but preferably a master's degree (a two-year, graduate-level degree that is earned after a student receives a bachelor's degree), to work as an engineer or scientist in the driverless vehicle industry. Technologists and technicians prepare for the field by earning an associate's degree (a degree that requires a two-year course of study after high school), but many have bachelors degrees. Once they graduate from college, some people go onto complete additional training via a short **apprenticeship**. Some aspiring autonomous vehicle industry professionals first receive computer, engineering, or scientific training in the military and then earn a **certificate** in AI, machine learning, or robotics, or take classes in these and other areas to build their skills. The following sections provide more information on educational preparation.

HIGH SCHOOL CLASSES

Start out by taking as many computer science classes as possible, including:
- Introduction to Computer Science
- Computer Programming
- Software Development
- Computer Security

Some high schools offer classes in robotics, AI, machine learning, and data science. Taking these courses if they're offered will provide you with great preparation for college study.

Mathematics provides the framework for AI and machine-learning software (the brains of driverless vehicles), so you should take the following classes to build your math skills:
- algebra
- trigonometry
- calculus
- linear algebra
- discrete mathematics
- applied mathematics
- statistics

Driverless vehicle developers frequently write about and discuss their work with colleagues, company executives, and sometimes the media. Take speech and writing classes to develop your communication skills. Be sure to take these courses seriously. Written communication skills are the number one ability

Take as many math classes as possible in high school and college.

hiring managers seek in new graduates, according to a survey by the National Association of Colleges and Employers. Oral communication skills ranked seventh out of twenty important traits cited by employers.

If you plan on pursuing a career in vehicle design (creating the exterior and interior look of driverless vehicles), take art and CAD classes.

Other useful high school classes include:
- physics
- engineering
- psychology (to help you understand how humans think)
- philosophy (to develop your critical-thinking skills)
- foreign language (especially if you plan to specialize in natural language processing and/or work outside your home country)
- business, marketing, and accounting (if you plan to start a company)

COLLEGES AND UNIVERSITIES

The self-driving vehicle industry is an interdisciplinary field, and its workers have degrees in many areas. Engineers and scientists have degrees in robotics and autonomous systems; computer science; software development; and computer, electrical, electronics, industrial, manufacturing, mechanical, software, or systems engineering. If you want to become a manager and/or get the best-paying jobs, you'll need to earn a master's degree in one of the previously mentioned fields, or a degree in business management or engineering management.

Technicians and technologists have an associate's degree in computer science or in robotics, computer, electrical, electronics, electro-mechanical, manufacturing,

A college student (left) works on a robotics project under the supervision of a teacher.

or mechanical engineering technology. Some employers may require that applicants for technician and technologist careers have a bachelor's degree.

A few colleges and universities have created degree programs in artificial intelligence or related fields. In 2018, Carnegie Mellon University (Pittsburgh, PA) became the first U.S. school to offer an undergraduate degree in AI. Indiana University at Bloomington offers a bachelor of science in intelligent systems engineering. In the United Kingdom, the University of Edinburgh offers a bachelor of science in AI.

The online learning platform Udacity offers an Introduction to Self-Driving Cars Nanodegree Program for students who do not have a background in autonomous vehicles. Students complete ten hours of study per week during the four-month academic term. Applicants should have some experience with algebra and programming (writing short scripts in any programming language). Udacity offers a variety of free courses that help students build these skills if they do not already have them. Graduates of Udacity's introductory program are guaranteed admission into its Self-Driving Car Engineer Nanodegree Program, which was created in cooperation with Mercedes-Benz, NVIDIA, Uber, BMW, and other companies that are developing driverless vehicle technology. The degree can be earned by completing fifteen hours of study per week during two, three-month terms. Participants must have intermediate proficiency in Python or C++ and basic knowledge of linear algebra, calculus, statistics, and physics. The program has eight courses:

- Introduction
- Computer Vision
- Deep Learning
- Sensor Fusion
- Localization
- Path Planning
- Control
- System Integration

DRIVERLESS VEHICLE TECHNOLOGY RESEARCH HOTSPOTS

The following colleges and universities conduct extensive research in autonomous and semi-autonomous vehicle technology. If you're interested in this field, you should check out programs offered by these schools.

- Massachusetts Institute of Technology (United States)
- Stanford University (United States)
- University of Michigan (United States)
- Oxford University (United Kingdom)
- Tsinghua University (China)
- Seoul National University (Korea)

College students typically complete at least one internship as part of their training. An internship is a paid or unpaid learning opportunity in which a student works at a business to get experience. It can last anywhere from a few weeks to a year.

DAY IN THE LIFE: DRIVERLESS VEHICLE DESIGNER

When fully autonomous vehicles are in wide use, their interiors and exteriors will look much different than those of conventional cars and trucks. In regard to the exterior of the car, designers will need to incorporate sensors, cameras, LiDAR, RADAR, and other components in such a way that they are both visually attractive and functional. This is an interesting field, but my specialty is the redesign of the interior area of vehicles.

Designing the interior involves much more than simply removing the wheel, brake and gas pedals, and other components that are necessary in a traditional vehicle. In an autonomous vehicle, the front and back seats are configured so that the passengers face each other. And perhaps they will be designed to swivel so that passengers can orient them however they want to. The air bags will need to be reoriented so that they protect passengers regardless of the direction they're facing. The lighting will be different, and heating and cooling vents will be oriented in a new way. As we imagine the future interior layout, we ask ourselves many questions. What type of enhanced entertainment features will be added now that there is no longer a human driver? Should we create targeted audio systems that can locate a passenger and deliver specialized entertainment? What about an alert system that reminds people in self-driving taxis to remove items they stored in a bin? What type of tables and other flat surfaces will we incorporate so that passengers can comfortably do work, have a snack, use their computers, and do many other tasks? What features will be included on the passenger-vehicle interface, and how will it look? How about projecting a movie onto the front windshield, or a social media feed on the side windows? How can we incorporate virtual and augmented reality into the passenger experience?

Really, the sky is the limit regarding what features we can add to the interior of an autonomous vehicle, and that's what gets me excited about my job. We're changing something that, in some ways, has been the same for 100 years. This is both a challenge and a really cool aspect of my job.

MILITARY

The U.S. military has been developing land-, water-, and air-based semi-autonomous and autonomous vehicles for years. It already uses unmanned aerial vehicles to conduct surveillance and wage war against terrorists and other enemies. Many military experts believe that driverless vehicles will be in use by the armed forces long before they are widely introduced on our roads and highways.

If you're interested in working in the driverless vehicle industry, the various branches of the U.S. military (Air Force, Army, Coast Guard, Marines, and Navy) offer a variety of computer-, engineering-, and math-related training opportunities. Some will give you direct experience with robotics (keep in mind that driverless vehicles are basically robots) and AI, while others will provide a good knowledge base that you can build on once you leave the military. The following military careers are a good option for those interested in preparing for a career in the self-driving vehicle industry:

- software developer
- computer programmer
- information security analyst
- electrical engineer
- electrical equipment and equipment repairer
- electronics engineer
- industrial engineer
- statistician
- mathematical technician
- intelligence specialist

Visit TodaysMilitary.com to learn more about these and other occupations. Militaries in other countries also provide computer, engineering, and

If you serve in the U.S. military, you may get the chance to help develop driverless vehicles, such as the U.S. Army's Autonomous Platform Demonstrator.

mathematics training. For example, you can learn more about careers in the Canadian armed forces by visiting www.canada.ca/en/department-national-defence/services/caf-jobs.html. Visit www.army.mod.uk/careers to learn more about opportunities in the British military.

If you enlist (agree to serve) in the military, you'll receive a salary and food and lodging and will not have to pay any tuition, but you will have to make a service commitment of two to four years.

GETTING A JOB

After you earn a degree or are discharged from the military, you'll need to get a job. While it's not yet time to enter the world of work, it's a good idea to get a basic understanding of how the job search process works. That way, when you start encountering terms such as "networking," "job boards," and "professional association," you'll be that much ahead of other job-seekers. Here are some popular job search methods.

The head of autonomous driving at Mercedes-Benz offers tips on breaking into the industry

USE YOUR NETWORK

"Your relationships with people like your family, friends, coworkers, classmates, former supervisors, faculty, etc. can play a valuable role in exploring careers, job searching, and moving up in your career," advises the Career Center at the University of Kentucky. When you interact with these and other types of people to advance your educational or career interests, this is called networking.

In addition to getting help from those you know, you can expand your network by meeting new people at career fairs, during internships, at competitions and camps, and any other place where people who are interested in driverless vehicle technology gather and discuss their interests in this emerging field. You can also interact with people you know, as well as make new contacts, by using LinkedIn and other social networking sites.

Start networking while you're in high school—and keep doing so while you're in college or the military. Tell people that you're interested in pursuing education and a career in driverless vehicle development to see if they can

Some of your high school and college classmates will become valuable members of your network.

provide suggestions on classes, college programs, camps, clubs, competitions, networking groups, and any other opportunity where you can expand your knowledge and skills.

CHECK OUT JOB BOARDS

Many professional associations, companies, and other organizations have internet job boards that list internship and job openings. While you're probably a few years from applying for an internship or job, it's a good idea to check out some listings to see what types of education and skills are in demand. Here are a few driverless vehicle job boards and company websites:

- www.driverless.global/jobs
- www.drive.ai/careers
- https://search-careers.gm.com/autonomous-jobs

And here are some general job sites that offer driverless vehicle development job listings.

- www.indeed.com
- www.linkedin.com
- www.dice.com
- www.cybercareers.gov/job-seeker (U.S. government job board)
- www.jobbank.gc.ca (Canadian government job board)
- www.gov.uk/jobsearch (United Kingdom government job board)

JOIN AND USE THE RESOURCES OF PROFESSIONAL ASSOCIATIONS

What is a professional association and what can it do for me, you might ask. First, a professional association is an organization that is founded by a group of people who have the same career (electrical engineers, computer security specialists, etc.) or who work in the same industry specialty (AI, robotics, driverless vehicles, etc.). The answer to question number two: A LOT! Professional associations provide membership (including categories for students), job listings, training opportunities, networking events, discussion boards, publications, and much more. There are thousands of professional associations around the world for people who work in robotics, AI, driverless vehicle technology, and related areas. Here are a few to check out. You can perform an internet keyword search to locate more organizations.

- Connected Vehicle Trade Association (international): www.connectedvehicle.org
- International Federation of Robotics: https://ifr.org
- IEEE Robotics and Automation Society (international): www.ieee-ras.org
- Robotic Industries Association (international): www.robotics.org
- The Institution of Engineering and Technology (United Kingdom): www.theiet.org

- Engineers Canada: https://engineerscanada.ca
- Engineers Australia: www.engineersaustralia.org.au

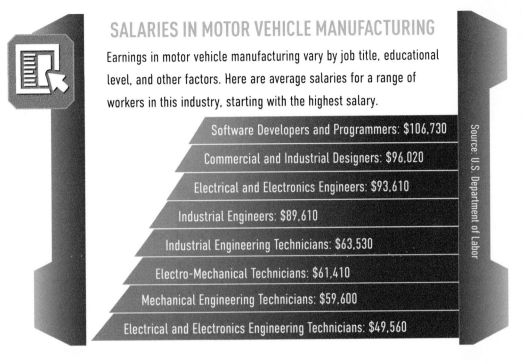

SALARIES IN MOTOR VEHICLE MANUFACTURING

Earnings in motor vehicle manufacturing vary by job title, educational level, and other factors. Here are average salaries for a range of workers in this industry, starting with the highest salary.

Software Developers and Programmers: $106,730

Commercial and Industrial Designers: $96,020

Electrical and Electronics Engineers: $93,610

Industrial Engineers: $89,610

Industrial Engineering Technicians: $63,530

Electro-Mechanical Technicians: $61,410

Mechanical Engineering Technicians: $59,600

Electrical and Electronics Engineering Technicians: $49,560

Source: U.S. Department of Labor

HOW MUCH CAN I EARN?

Earnings for driverless vehicle developers vary by educational background, their level of experience, employer, location, whether they work full or part time, and other criteria. Autonomous vehicle developers earn average salaries of $138,000 a year, according to Paysa.com, a website that uses machine learning to collect salary information. It also reports that autonomous vehicle engineers receive an average of $238,018, with salaries ranging from $173,198 to more than $356,565. These salary numbers include a **base salary**, stock options (an option to buy stock—a tiny amount of ownership in the company—at a set price within a set time period), and **bonuses**.

Self-driving vehicle test operators earn anywhere from $20 to $25 an hour, according to job listings for these positions.

There is not a ton of information available regarding salaries in the driverless vehicle industry, so let's take a look at earnings for the AI workers who play a major role in this field.

Machine-learning engineers earn salaries that range from $76,190 to $153,030, according to PayScale.com. They receive average bonuses of $10,174 and average **profit sharing** of $16,500.

Big data engineers earn salaries that ranged from $127,250 to $219,500, according to Robert Half Technology's *Salary Guide for Technology Professionals*. Salaries for data scientists ranged from $102,750 to $175,000.

Salaries in AI research are much higher. AI specialists with little or no industry experience can earn between $300,000 and $500,000 a year in salary and stock options, according to the *New York Times (NYT)*. Top AI researchers at private research labs at tech companies are paid $1 million or more. "Salaries for top AI

Software developers earn average salaries that are much higher than the average for all workers.

researchers have skyrocketed because there are not many people who understand the technology and thousands of companies want to work with it," according to the *NYT*. In 2018, Element AI, an independent lab in Canada, estimated that only 22,000 people worldwide had the skills required to conduct serious AI research.

Driverless vehicle developers who work full time (35–40 hours a week) for companies and other organizations often receive fringe benefits such as health insurance, paid vacation and sick days, and other perks. Freelancers do not receive these benefits. A freelancer is a type of worker who does not work full time for a company or organization, but who provides services as needed. They do not receive a regular salary or fringe benefits, but are paid by the hour or project.

TEXT-DEPENDENT QUESTIONS:

1. What high school classes should you take to prepare for a career in driverless vehicle development?
2. What is a professional association?
3. What is the average salary for driverless vehicle professionals?

RESEARCH PROJECT:

Visit some of the job boards listed in this chapter and locate employment listings for three different driverless vehicle development careers (such as engineers, technicians, and AI developers). Compare and contrast the job duties, educational requirements, and preferred skills for these careers, and write a 500-word report that summarizes your findings. Which career is the best for you, and why?

WORDS TO UNDERSTAND

bootcamp: a short-term, highly focused learning opportunity in which participants are taught the most important aspects of a complicated topic, such as coding

embedded software: a specialized type of software that is used to control non-computer devices such as those in the automotive, health-care, and aviation industries

job shadowing: observing a worker as they do their job in order to learn more about a specific career

national laboratory: a research institution established by the U.S. government during World War II to conduct cutting-edge research; there are seventeen national laboratories that are operated by the U.S. Department of Energy

KEY SKILLS AND METHODS OF EXPLORATION

SKILL BUILDING LEADS TO SUCCESS

You'll need a wide variety of technical knowledge and personal skills to be a successful driverless vehicle developer. Indeed.com recently conducted a study of autonomous vehicle development job listings and identified the following as the most important abilities for success for those working in computer science and engineering positions:

1. Programming: C or C++
2. Programming: Python
3. Image processing

4. Artificial intelligence
5. Machine learning
6. Programming tools: Git
7. Programming: MATLAB
8. Programming: Java
9. Programming: Shell script
10. **Embedded software**

DID YOU KNOW?

The information technology staffing firm Robert Half Technology included AI and machine learning, as well as several programming languages and tools used in these fields, on its list of "In-demand Technical Skills and Expertise."

Your skill set will vary based on your profession, but computer skills are the top of the list for most driverless vehicle development careers. Additionally, you should have a strong background in mathematics (including having knowledge of statistics, linear algebra, mathematical optimization, and probability). Proficiency in these and other technical areas are extremely important in this industry, but you'll also need soft skills to be successful. Here are some key soft skills:

- interpersonal and communication skills
- problem-solving skills
- willingness to continue learning
- judgment and decision-making skills
- detail-oriented

- logical thinking ability
- creativity
- curiosity
- problem-solving ability
- passion
- self-motivation
- ability to multitask and meet deadlines
- time-management
- leadership (if you work in management or own a business)
- business skills (if you decide to launch a business)

Students in a high school robotics club.

CHANGING SKILL SETS FOR ENGINEERS

"Unlike today's engineers who typically work on specific automotive components, such as engines or electronics, the interconnected nature of future automotive systems will require engineers who are cross-functional 'tinkerers,' who have a strong foundation in mathematics and physics; deep skills in artificial intelligence, machine learning, robotics, data sciences, and software; and a passion for cars."

Sources: Boston Consulting Group and Detroit Mobility Lab

EXPLORING DRIVERLESS VEHICLE DEVELOPMENT AS A STUDENT

There are many ways to learn more about self-driving cars and careers in the field. Here are some popular methods of exploration.

START A CLUB

Your middle school or high school may already have an engineering, mathematics, robotics, or computer science club. If so, that's great. Such clubs allow you to experiment with and build machines and develop technology, meet people who have the same interests, learn more about potential career paths (through presentations by engineers and scientists, visits to companies, and other opportunities), and much more. Maybe you could even start a driverless vehicle development club. That's what students at a California high school did. They even built a 1:10 scale model of a self-driving car by using open-source code and off-the-shelf parts and electrical components. If no such club exists at your school, start one! Ask your science or math teacher for help getting organized.

DID YOU KNOW?

Seventy percent of Americans surveyed by the Consumer Technology Association said that they want to test a self-driving car.

TAKE A CLASS

You'll take plenty of science, math, and engineering classes in school, but you can also sign up for online and in-person courses that are offered by private organizations, professional associations, and other providers. These courses will give you a good introduction to different fields (such as AI, robotics, computer security, etc.) and learn what career or careers would be a good fit for your interests. Some courses are even free. For example, Udacity offers Intro to Artificial Intelligence, a free online class that takes about four months to complete. The class covers topics such as robotics, computer vision, machine learning, and natural language processing.

Coursera.org is another well-known provider of classes. Some of its recent courses include:

- Algorithms
- Launching Into Machine Learning
- Introduction to TensorFlow for Artificial Intelligence

JOIN THE TECHNOLOGY STUDENT ASSOCIATION (TSA)

If you're a middle school or high school student and interested in science, technology, engineering, and mathematics, consider joining the TSA (www.tsaweb.org). This national nonprofit organization offers sixty competitions at its annual conference—including those in coding, software development, engineering design, CAD engineering, system control technology, and technology problem-solving. (A nonprofit organization is a group that uses any profits it generates to advance its stated goals. It is not a corporation or other for-profit business.) The TSA also provides opportunities to develop your leadership skills and compete for money for college. Ask your school counselor or science teacher if your school has a TSA chapter and, if not, ask them to start one.

ATTEND A SUMMER CAMP

Camps are available in a wide range of areas that are related to driverless vehicle development—from general math, engineering, and computer science to more specialized areas such as robotics, AI, and computer security. Residential and day camps are available. At most residential camps, you won't sleep in a tent, but in a college dormitory or other comfortable building. Camps last anywhere from a few days to a few weeks. Some are free, while others require a program fee that covers camp activities, food and lodging, and other expenses. Scholarships are sometimes available that pay for all or some of the cost of attendance.

Your school counselor or computer science or math teacher can direct you toward opportunities in your area. Here are some well-known camps in the United States and Canada. Camps are also available in other countries.

MASSACHUSETTS INSTITUTE OF TECHNOLOGY
BEAVER WORKS SUMMER INSTITUTE

Students who will be entering their senior year in high school can participate in this four-week program that teaches STEM skills through project-based, workshop-style courses. Class topics change each year. Recent courses included Autonomous RaceCar, Autonomous Air Vehicle Racing, Autonomous Cognitive Assistance, Embedded Security and Hardware Hacking, and Unmanned Air System–Synthetic Aperture RADAR. Learn more at https://beaverworks.ll.mit.edu/CMS/bw/bwsi.

CAMP PROVIDERS

- colleges and universities

- high schools

- community groups

- private tech and science organizations

- government science agencies

- science and technology museums

iDTech

Each year, iDTech hosts more than 60,000 residential campers ages seven to nineteen at 150 colleges and universities in the United States and several other countries. Its Autonomous and Self-Driving Robotics Lab lasts two weeks and is held in ten U.S. states, the District of Columbia, and the United Kingdom. Participants—who must be between the ages of thirteen and eighteen—will learn the fundamentals of electrical engineering, explore computer vision and autonomous robotics, learn how to code with Arduino and MicroPython, develop their logical thinking skills, and build their own autonomous robot that they can take home. Programs are also available in AI and machine learning, coding, robotics, and cybersecurity. These are fee-based camps. Learn more at www.idtech.com.

DAY IN THE LIFE: SOFTWARE ENGINEER

I've worked as a software engineer for ten years. I started out writing code for video games, but as the field of artificial intelligence (AI) field emerged, I caught the AI bug and signed up for Udacity's Self-Driving Car Engineer Nanodegree Program to expand my skills. My fascination with AI, combined with my lifelong interest in automotives (I was one of the only girls in my high school's automotive club), steered me toward a career in the driverless vehicle industry, where I've worked for four years.

Each day varies based on what stage we're at in a project. I might work on localization software that allows the vehicle to determine exactly where it is in the world and on the road with the help of sensors, GPS, and maps. We use algorithms to estimate where the vehicle is within an error margin of less than 4 inches (about 10 centimeters). Another day, I'll work on path planning (how the car gets to a destination, predicting what other vehicles will do on the road, and developing a plan to interact with these other vehicles and other challenges to safely arrive at the destination). We also brainstorm ideas to create new software or improve the performance of existing programs.

While I love writing and troubleshooting code, I really enjoy testing the software in the vehicles. We have testers that take the cars out on the road, but we also get to plug our laptops into the dashboard and monitor the car's performance as it travels on a test track. It's really neat to be able to see in real-time what is working well and what needs improvement.

There are a lot of software engineers in the world, but not too many that get the chance to be part of a brand-new industry. That's why I love my job and look forward to the day when an autonomous vehicle I helped write the code for is in regular use on our streets and highways. Someday, I'll be able to point to a driverless car on the road and say, "I helped make that!"

AI4ALL

AI4ALL is a nonprofit organization that seeks to increase diversity and inclusion in artificial intelligence. It partners with the following universities to offer summer programs in AI and related areas for teens:

- Arizona State University
- Boston University
- Carnegie Mellon University
- Columbia University
- Princeton University
- Simon Fraser University

- Stanford University
- University of California at Berkeley
- University of California at San Francisco
- University of Maryland

Visit AI4ALL's website, http://ai-4-all.org/education, to learn about each university's program, start dates, and other information.

SOURCES OF ADDITIONAL EXPLORATION

Contact the following organizations for more information on education and careers in driverless vehicle development:

Association for Computing Machinery Special Interest Group in Artificial Intelligence
www.acm.org/special-interest-groups/sigs/sigai

Association for the Advancement of Artificial Intelligence
www.aaai.org

Australia and New Zealand Driverless Vehicle Initiative (ANZDVI)
https://advi.org.au

Canadian Artificial Intelligence Association
www.caiac.ca

Connected Vehicle Trade Association
www.connectedvehicle.org

IEEE Robotics and Automation Society
www.ieee-ras.org

International Federation of Robotics
https://ifr.org

International Society of Automation
www.isa.org

Robotic Industries Association
www.robotics.org

SAE International
www.sae.org

NATIONAL STUDENT LEADERSHIP CONFERENCE (NSLC)

The NSLC offers a nine-day summer engineering program for high school students that is held two to four times each summer in six U.S. cities. If you participate in this program, you'll learn about mechanical, civil, electrical, mechanical, and other engineering specialties. You'll design, build, and operate a remotely operated underwater vehicle. And you'll get a chance to talk with a variety of professionals who will help you learn more about careers in engineering. The NSLC also offers a cybersecurity program. Learn more at www.nslcleaders.org/youth-leadershipprograms/engineering-summer-programs.

DIGITAL MEDIA ACADEMY

The academy offers a one-week Autonomous Arduino with Take-Home Robot Camp for young people ages twelve to seventeen at locations throughout the United States and Canada. In this camp, you'll learn how to program in Arduino Signal processing, build electronic circuits, and troubleshoot errors and solve problems with an end goal of building a robot that performs autonomous tasks. The academy also offers programs in AI and machine learning, data science, and programming. Learn more at www. digitalmediaacademy.org.

FINDING MORE CAMPS

Many other colleges, businesses, and other organizations offer summer camps. Contact schools and organizations in your area to learn more.

PARTICIPATE IN A COMPETITION

Associations, colleges and universities, tech and automotive companies, high schools, and other organizations sponsor contests that allow you to test your skills and knowledge against others who are interested in driverless vehicle technology, AI, programming, and robotics. Check out the following competitions:

HIGH SCHOOL AUTONOMOUS VEHICLE CHALLENGE

The Rose-Hulman Institute of Technology in Terre Haute, Indiana, offers the Autonomous Vehicle Challenge to student teams from all over the United States. Competitors must assemble a vehicle kit, create autonomous vehicle algorithms that are similar to those used by Ford Motor Company, and then race their vehicles against other teams. The team with the fastest vehicle that stays on the racetrack wins. The competition is sponsored by Ford Motor Company, The MathWorks, and NXP Semiconductors. Learn more at www.rose-hulman.edu/academics/educational-outreach/ autonomous-vehicle-challenge.

AUTONOMOUS VEHICLE COMPETITION

Argonne **National Laboratory** in Lemont, Illinois, offers an Autonomous Vehicle Competition for high school students. Teams are required to design and program an autonomous vehicle that can travel through a maze-like obstacle course in a designated amount of time, and with the least

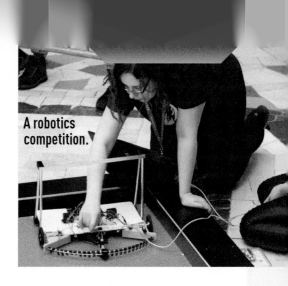

A robotics competition.

amount of human assistance. Teams are judged on their engineering design process, vehicle design, and vehicle performance. Learn more at www.anl. gov/education/high-school-autonomous-vehicle-competition.

THE NATIONAL AUTOMOTIVE TECHNOLOGY COMPETITION

The National Automotive Technology Competition is not geared for those who want to develop driverless technology, but for those who are interested in repairing traditional vehicles. It is held each year at the New York International Auto Show. High school teams from around the United States first participate in state- and regional-level contests to determine the top students from each location. The competition takes place over two days. On day one, contestants are tested on their knowledge of tools, measuring instruments, specific vehicle components, and job interview skills. On day two, each two-person student team must diagnose and repair a number of preassigned problems under a car's hood in a certain amount of time. In a recent year, more than $3 million in prizes and scholarships were awarded to participating students and schools. Learn more at www. nationalautotechcompetition.com.

WORLD ARTIFICIAL INTELLIGENCE COMPETITION FOR YOUTH

This competition is open to students from age four to twenty. Students first participate in a four-day workshop that provides an overview of AI and toolkits that will prepare them to compete in a regional competition. Winners of the regional competition compete at the national level. Each year, the competition has a new theme. One recent theme was "How to Make the World Better with AI." Learn more at www.readyai.org/waicy.

BATTLECODE

Battlecode is a programming competition that is offered by the Massachusetts Institute of Technology. High school and college students can participate in this challenge, which combines battle strategy, software engineering, and AI. A total of $50,000 in prizes is available. Learn more at www.battlecode.org.

SkillsUSA

SkillsUSA is a national membership organization for middle school, high school, and college students who are preparing for careers in technical, trade, and skilled service occupations. It offers several competitions for those who are interested in computers and other technology. Competitions include Automotive Service Technology, Computer Programming, Electronics Technology, Engineering Technology/Design, Mechatronics, Mobile Robotics Technology, Principles of Engineering/Technology, Related Technical Math, and Robotics and Automation Technology. SkillsUSA works directly with high schools and colleges, so ask your school counselor or teacher if it is an option for you. Learn more at www.skillsusa.org.

Watch students prepare
for and compete in the
High School Autonomous
Vehicle Project

OTHER COMPETITIONS

Here are some additional contests to investigate:

- BEST Robotics Competitions: www.bestinc.org
- VEX Robotics Competitions: www.vexrobotics.com/vexedr/competition
- FIRST Robotics Competition: www.firstinspires.org
- National Science Bowl: www.science.energy.gov/wdts/nsb
- Skills Compétences Canada: www.skillscompetencescanada.com

OTHER WAYS TO LEARN MORE ABOUT
SELF-DRIVING VEHICLES

- Attend driverless vehicle development (DVD) conferences
- Visit science and technology museums
- Participate in DVD discussion boards online
- Do basic maintenance tasks on your family's car to get a general understanding of how vehicles work

- Attend a coding bootcamp
- Join the Boy Scouts or Girls Scouts (they offer merit badges in Robotics, Engineering, Computer Science, and related fields)
- Watch videos about DVD
- Start a DVD or robotics, engineering, or software development club
- Try creating an algorithm
- Participate in an information interview with DVD workers in which you ask them questions about their job duties, educational preparation, key skills for success, and other topics to help you learn more about the field
- Job shadow a DVD professional
- Talk to your school counselor about career opportunities in DVD
- Work with your school counselor or computer science teacher to organize a tech career fair

A collegiate coding competition.

Students participate in an autonomous and electric vehicle competition at the Museum of Science and Industry in Chicago, IL.

TEXT-DEPENDENT QUESTIONS:

1. Can you name five key soft skills for driverless vehicle developers?
2. What is the Beaver Works Summer Institute?
3. What is SkillsUSA?

RESEARCH PROJECT:

Try to write a basic algorithm. Perform a keyword search on "how to write an algorithm" and check out YouTube.com for tips to get started. The following website offers several good ideas and some free resources: https://thenextweb. com/artificial-intelligence/2018/08/02/a-beginners-guide-to-ai-algorithms. When you're done, show your algorithm to your computer teacher and ask for feedback.

WORDS TO UNDERSTAND

feasible: the degree of being easily or conveniently done

logistics companies: those that oversee the delivery of goods from one location to another

revenue: money earned from the sales of goods or services

mass transportation: the movement of large groups of people within urban areas by using buses, trains, and other group travel technologies; also known as **mass transit** and **public transportation**

Chapter 5

THE FUTURE OF DRIVERLESS VEHICLE TECHNOLOGY AND CAREERS

THE BIG PICTURE

Driverless vehicles will eventually come into widespread usage. When this technology is perfected, there will be the potential for less traffic congestion, a reduced risk of injury to humans and damage to vehicles, and many other benefits. But the timeline for when fully autonomous will be introduced is uncertain because of concerns about safety, the need to upgrade road infrastructure, challenges with technology, and other factors. Industry experts believe that fully autonomous vehicles will first be introduced en masse in specialized industries such as agriculture, mining, and **mass transportation**. Other transportation experts predict that self-driving cars will operate in some areas (such as on highways), but not others. Dedicated lanes for self-driving vehicles may need to be created until all the technological bugs are addressed.

But in the next decade, automakers and tech companies will continue to increase the level of autonomy of vehicles with a goal of reaching complete autonomy. The growing number of companies that are developing self-driving technology demonstrates that this technology is here to stay and that there will be many new career opportunities. "Self-driving and electric cars will help create more than 100,000 U.S. mobility industry jobs in the coming decade,

Driverless vehicles will play a major role in agriculture because there is a shortage of farm laborers in many countries.

including up to 30,000 jobs for engineers with degrees in computer-related subjects," according to research from Boston Consulting Group and Detroit Mobility Lab. "But the demand could be as much as six times the expected number of such graduates, exacerbating the industry's already significant talent shortage." This research finds that an additional 65,000 jobs for skilled trades workers (automated and electric vehicle mechanics and safety drivers) could also be created.

AI is one of the key technologies that will allow semi-autonomous and autonomous vehicles to safely navigate our roadways. Without it, there would be no driverless vehicle industry. As a result, the employment outlook for AI professionals is excellent. "AI experts have become some of the most in-demand and best-paid talent in today's technological marketplace," according to Beatriz Remeseiro, assistant professor in the computer science department at the University of Oviedo, Spain, who was interviewed about the field by *Science*.

While the development of self-driving cars is creating jobs, it will also lead to significant job losses for truck, taxi, bus, and delivery drivers. Employment experts and politicians are working hard to address this issue and develop retraining programs for these workers. The transition for these employees will not be easy, but it mirrors the situation for workers in many other industries across the world who are losing their jobs as a result of technology and automation.

Although the introduction of driverless vehicles will cause job losses, it will also create new opportunities. The Australia and New Zealand Driverless Vehicle Initiative (ANZDVI) has identified the following areas that will benefit from the use of autonomous vehicles:

- **Electronics and software:** the value of software incorporated into vehicles is expected to quadruple

- **Trucking and freight movement:** freight capacity will increase for logistics companies, which will allow for more shipments; some drivers will transition to the role of monitoring the functioning of autonomous driving systems

- **Land and urban development:** land and city planners will be needed to transition unneeded parking spaces and, perhaps, land areas regained from the shrinking of the width of streets, to parks, housing, and other uses

- **Digital media:** demand for content (books, movies, television shows, news, etc.) will most likely increase because former drivers will seek entertainment options as they travel to and from destinations

For driverless vehicles to become a success, the technology that allows them to read and interpret road signs will have to be perfected.

DRIVERLESS VEHICLE PREDICTIONS

- The sale of self-driving vehicles may generate $87 billion in revenue by 2030.

- Ninety-two percent of autonomous vehicles will be at the Level 2 stage in 2030. These vehicles feature driver support features such as lane departure warnings, remote-controlled parking, collision avoidance braking, and adaptive cruise control technology that are available at the same time, but which are not fully autonomous.

- Eight percent of vehicles will be at the Level 3 stage in 2030. In these vehicles, automated driving features such as traffic jam chauffeur are available, but the human driver must take over in a matter of seconds when the system makes a request.

Source: Lux Research

CHALLENGES TO THE DEVELOPMENT OF DRIVERLESS TECHNOLOGY

There is no doubt that fully autonomous vehicles will eventually make up the majority of vehicles on our streets and highways, but the actual year in which this will happen is very uncertain because the industry still must overcome many road infrastructure, technology, safety, and other challenges. Here are a few issues that developers will need to master in order for fully automated—and even highly advanced semi-autonomous—vehicles to become widely available.

TECHNOLOGY AND COST ISSUES

Developers have made great technological advances as they design and build self-driving vehicles, but they have yet to overcome many roadblocks. Additionally, much of this technology is very expensive and it is not **feasible** yet to use it in mass-produced vehicles. For example, LiDAR, required in many driverless vehicles, is very costly ($75,000 to $85,000 per unit) and is not ready to be integrated into mass-produced driverless vehicles. Self-driving algorithms, sensors, LiDAR, RADAR, and other technology can currently be confused by too much activity on the streets, night driving conditions, bad weather, very sunny conditions, and potholes.

Learn about ten ways that autonomous cars will redefine the future

MAPPING CHALLENGES

For driverless vehicles to work effectively, they need extremely accurate 3–D maps that can help them navigate busy streets and highways. These maps must be constantly updated, and tech companies are working on ways to produce better maps. Additionally, maps of rural areas are generally poor, and they will need updating in order for driverless vehicles to perform effectively.

ROAD INFRASTRUCTURE

Many difficulties still exist regarding how driverless vehicles will navigate roads effectively and safely. Street signs may need to be standardized, worn-off pavement markings will need to be repainted, and connected infrastructure will need to be built so that driverless vehicles can communicate with the world around them. These changes will be costly and time-consuming.

SAFETY

Even though nearly 40,000 people die in traffic accidents in the United States each year, many people still believe that conventional cars are much safer than driverless vehicles. The industry will need to find ways to educate the public about autonomous vehicles and, most importantly, reduce or completely

Driverless vehicle safety concerns the public, who don't wish to see accidents occur, such as this typical "human-driver" accident.

eliminate accidents and deaths caused by self-driving technology. Getting the public on board is key to the development of driverless vehicles.

IN CONCLUSION

Do you have excellent programming skills, enjoy solving problems, and are fascinated by the idea of developing driverless vehicles? Do you have a lot of "drive" and ambition? Are you looking to work in a field that offers high pay and excellent job prospects? If so, then a career in driverless vehicle development could be in your future.

I hope that you'll use this book as a starting point to discover even more about careers in the driverless vehicle industry. Talk to DVD professionals about their jobs, use the resources of professional organizations, attend summer camps,

A Mitsubishi electric autonomous driving system is field tested in Silicon Valley.

participate in competitions, and most importantly, learn how to create and use algorithms, write code, and build robots. Taking these and other steps will allow you to be part of one of the most exciting fields that has come down the occupational highway in years. Good luck on your career exploration!

TEXT-DEPENDENT QUESTIONS:

1. Why is demand strong for driverless vehicle industry professionals?
2. What factors might slow the growth of the driverless vehicle industry?
3. Can you name three ways that driverless vehicle technology will change society in the future?

RESEARCH PROJECT:

Expand on your answer to question #3 above. Are all of these changes good, or could there be some drawbacks to this technology that we may not even have imagined yet? Write a report that details why you think the use of driverless vehicles could be both a good and bad thing, and present it to your class.

Baine, Celeste. *Is There an Engineer Inside You?: A Comprehensive Guide to Career Decisions in Engineering*. 5th ed. Clarkesville, GA: Engineering Education Service Center, 2016.

Greer, Paul. STEM *Careers: A Student's Guide to Opportunities in Science, Technology, Engineering and Maths*. Bath, United Kingdom: Trotman Education, 2018.

Lipson, Hod, and Melba Kurma. *Driverless: Intelligent Cars and the Road Ahead*. Cambridge, MA: The MIT Press, 2016.

Mueller, John. *Artificial Intelligence For Dummies*. Hoboken, NJ: For Dummies, 2018.

Schauer, Pete (ed.) *Self-Driving Cars*. New York: Greenhaven Publishing, 2018.

INTERNET RESOURCES

www.bls.gov/ooh: The *Occupational Outlook Handbook* is a U.S. Department of Labor publication that features information on job duties, educational requirements, salaries, and the employment outlook for computer and information research scientists, computer programmers, software developers, hardware engineers, electrical and electronics engineers, electro-mechanical technicians, mechanical engineers, electrical and electronics engineering technicians, and other STEM careers.

www.ucsusa.org/clean-vehicles/how-self-driving-cars-work: Learn how self-driving cars work.

www.wired.com/story/guide-self-driving-cars: Visit this website to read The *WIRED* Guide to Self-Driving Cars.

https://waymo.com: Waymo, a major self-driving car developer, explains what's involved in creating this type of vehicle.

www.nhtsa.gov/technology-innovation/automated-vehicles-safety: This resource from the National Highway Traffic Safety Administration offers information on automated safety technologies, the five levels of vehicle autonomy, and the benefits of vehicle automation, as well as answers to frequently asked questions about driverless vehicles.

VIDEO LINKS

Chapter 1:

Learn more about the five levels of autonomy for self-driving cars and the pros and cons of this technology: http://x-qr.net/1LNd

Take a ride in Waymo's self-driving car: http://x-qr.net/1KJE

Chapter 3:

The head of autonomous driving at Mercedes-Benz offers tips on breaking into the industry: http://x-qr.net/1JXy

Chapter 4:

Watch students prepare for and compete in the High School Autonomous Vehicle Project: http://x-qr.net/1KeL

Chapter 5:

Learn about ten ways that autonomous cars will redefine the future: http://x-qr.net/1LqD

AUTHOR BIOGRAPHY

Andrew Morkes has been a writer and editor for more than twenty-five years. He is the author of more than twenty-five books about college-planning and careers, including all of the titles in this series, many titles in the *Careers in the Building Trades* series, *the Vault Career Guide to Social Media*, and *They Teach That in College!?: A Resource Guide to More Than 100 Interesting College Majors*, which was selected as one of the best books of the year by the library journal *Voice of Youth Advocates*. He is also the author and publisher of "The Morkes Report: College and Career Planning Trends" blog.